By a woman who finds excitement in your life and
financial success, fueled by a mindset of passion
and prosperity.

Clean A Smile

Change YOUR Life

Stephanie Welker

MY STORY

I began my dental career in early 2000's by searching for the quickest and most practical schooling option that would still provide a meaningful benefit. That search led me to a trade school for medical students: I chose Dental Assisting. The program lasted ten months, running Monday through Thursday, which allowed me to work double shifts at a convenience store on Fridays, Saturdays, and Sundays.

After completing my training, I was drawn to the more hands-on, surgical side of dentistry thereby choosing to work in an Oral and Maxillofacial Office. My experience in the field grew rapidly and, in many directions giving me valuable skills and knowledge. Even though I was excelling and loving the surgery indusrty, as time went on, I found myself frustrated— working tirelessly but was not seeing the level of compensation I truly wanted. It's not that I wasn't earning a good salary—I was. But it seemed as though no matter how high I climbed the in-office, multi-practice, technology-driven career ladder, I would eventually hit a ceiling in both pay and professional growth—in spite of having every surgical in-office certification and training available—short of going back to school: I obtained my Emergency Medical Services Certification, Dental Anesthesia Assistant National Certification, Radiology Cert., Botox/Fillers Cert, and other credentials that allowed me to take on multiple roles within the OMS office, including management. But I still felt I was capable of more and aimed to reach a higher level of financial success.

Keep in mind, this was early 2000's and when most dental practices in the DMV area were still privately owned—higher pay and benefits were scarce. While I was expanding my skills and seizing every opportunity that came my way, I also enrolled in evening classes at the local community college with the goal of becoming a Dental Hygienist. I wanted more freedom and a higher salary, and I thought this was the only way to move up in the dental field.

After being accepted into the program, I made it to my third semester before walking away. And when I say "walked away," I mean I had a moment. Right there in the middle of clinicals, I dropped my instruments, said, "Fuck this," grabbed my shit, and walked out—just like that.

I can be a little hotheaded, and my strict instructor insisted that I use my right hand during the instrumentation exams. Since I'm ambidextrous, I felt more comfortable switching between my left and right hand depending on the angle. She felt more comfortable failing me than allowing me to use both hands. By the third semester of us going back and forth on this subject, I had enough.

At the time, I was furious. After four years of evening classes—balancing a full-time job, and raising two daughters, I had poured so much time, energy, and money into this path. I worked hard to get accepted into Hygiene School, took on loans for loupes, dental instrument kits, and everything else that came with it—only to be held back over something that did not affect my ability to do the work. I was furious at her for what I thought was being ridiculous, and at myself for allowing something so miniscule to bother me to the point of giving up everything I had worked so hard for. Either way, at that point, in my head, the bridge was burned.

But as always, life had a bigger plan than I could see. In the end, I landed an incredible position in dental sales.

I feel that is where my true Dental Story began.

Little humor for ya: You can see the attitude in my facial expression. Sheesh (lol)

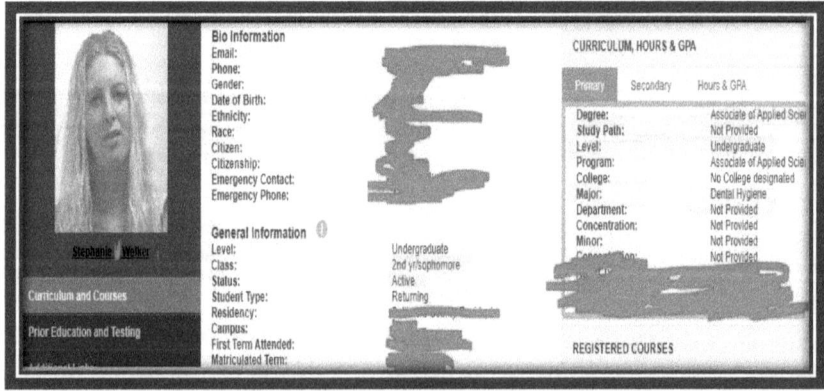

YOUR STORY

W hether you're currently in hygiene school or an experienced Dental Hygienist, you have invested time and effort into pursuing your dreams. You either made it happen or are in the thick of it to make it happen. You're the one who controls your emotions cnough to set a goal then follow through, regardless of the challenges that come with it. And that, my friend, is something to be extremely proud of. It means you have a goal-oriented mindset. You show up for yourself. You have the discipline to create real change in your life. It proves that you're striving for more—more growth, more opportunities, and a greater impact. So, regardless what stage you are in, don't downplay your accomplishments.

The question is: **Where do you go from here?**

THE PEP TALK

D on't overlook or underestimate the opportunities you have as a Dental Hygienist. You have a skill set and a license that essentially allows you to run your own business. You manage your own patients, operate in your own space, and in many states, you can create your schedule without the direct supervision from a licensed dentist. So, don't sell yourself short. Just as a dentist holds a professional title, so do you. Start viewing your title with the same level of respect and confidence you would if you were running your own business.

The first step in treating your career like a business is knowing you are a Licensed Dental Professional— your bank account should reflect your time, effort, and dedication it took to earn that title. Period.

"The only person you are destined
to become is the person
you decide to be."

-    Ralph Waldo Emerson

A Guide to Running Your Dental Hygiene Business

Table of Contents

Section 1-Building You

Section 2-Building Your Bank Account

Section 3-Becoming Unstoppable

SECTION ONE:

Know Who You Are &

What You Want

SECTION 1

<u>Life After Hygiene</u>

I n life, just as in dentistry, we shape the outcome from the very beginning. When we set goals, we are defining the results we want to achieve. Once we have an understanding of what we truly want, we take the necessary steps to make it happen. Without that clear vision, success is not impossible—we cannot accomplish what we have not defined. In essence,

Our entire life is built on the foundation that the outcome is shaped from the beginning.

The difference between the wealthy and the average American is in the design of their life. Some people move strategically, while others drift through their daily grind, caught in a cycle of complaints—whether about their job, their environment, the weather, the traffic, or life's hardships.

You may still have the occasional frustration, but you are already above average because you made the choice of becoming a Licensed Professional. Your title grants you the opportunity to achieve financial freedom, a core part of the American Dream.

Financial freedom looks different to everyone because our goals and dreams are personal to us. You get to define what financial freedom means to you. Maybe it is paying off your car note, owning a home free and clear by age 55, or purchasing a beautiful beach house in southern Florida or Brazil. The height of our achievements has no limitations. You decide.

Perhaps financial freedom, for you, means having the option to stop working on your terms—supported by your investments, passive income, and the interest earned from your savings.

It is a matter of figuring out:

➢ What do you want out of life?
➢ How much money do you want to earn?

- ➤ Why did you choose to become a Hygienist?
- ➤ What are your personal and professional goals?
- ➤ Do you want the freedom to retire on your terms?
- ➤ What fuels your determination to accomplish your goals?
  - Money
  - Family
  - To prove to yourself you can?
- ➤ Are you willing to,
  - Explore financial investments
  - Learn passive income opportunities
  - Create strategies to maintain a solid savings routine?

As you reflect on these questions, your answers should come quickly and naturally; those responses will guide your next steps, helping you understand what to focus on and what truly interests you. They are meant to be guides to make you realize that you are in control of your career, your personal growth, and your financial future. Your life will transform when you decide what you want and begin to view yourself as a Business Professional. The way you carry yourself directly influences how others perceive you—when you project confidence and professionalism, people will respond accordingly.

Life After Hygiene is designed to inspire you and shift your perspective on both your personal life and profession. This is the beginning of your new journey—one that you are about to embark on with intention and purpose.

As we move through the chapters of this book, set your standards, decide what you want out of life then define your business goals based on the outcome of what your vision is for your personal goals.

<u>**You set your standards**</u>

View yourself as the Business Professional that you are, not "just a" Dental Hygienist—others will follow.

<u>Life After Hygiene: Goals</u>

Why did you become a Dental Hygienist?

_____

_____

_____

How much money do you want to make?

_____

_____

Is your goal to become financially free, or do you plan on working until retirement age?

_____

_____

If you had all the money you desired, how would you spend your days?

_____

_____

_____

_____

_____

"If opportunity doesn't knock, build a door"
- Milton Berle

Personal Goals

Business is business, and pleasure is pleasure: Learn to compartmentalize to maintain balance between the two. During work hours, be fully engaged. Work hard. Work efficiently. And if needed, set aside 5 to 30 minutes at the end of your day to organize your to-do list for the next day, reflect on the day's events, or clear your mind—whatever helps you leave work with a sense of completion.

In other words, once your workday ends, leave it behind. If necessary, allow yourself a block of quiet time on your commute home. After that, release the day's thoughts until returning to work the next morning. The same principle applies in reverse—when you're at work, be fully present. Learn to control your thoughts regarding your life outside of business.

Ask yourself these two very crucial questions,

1. When I am at work, is there anything I can do about what's happening in my personal life?
2. When I am at home, is there anything I can do about what's happening at work?

The answer to both: NO, you cannot.

You can pause work to handle personal stuff but you cannot do both at the same time. So, learn to compartmentalize, I promise implementing this will become your best friend. And, you're welcome—I just added ten years to your life, just kidding. But in all seriousness, learn to compartmentalize different matters, you cannot be fully present if your mind is elsewhere. This includes when out to dinner with the fam, when spending time with the ladies or gents, kid time, and virtually all aspects of your life: Learn to be present, doing only what you can do in that moment. Otherwise, jot it down or set a reminder in your phone then carry on with what you are doing.

The goal is to be the best version of yourself in both your personal and professional life.

When you achieve that balance, success follows in both areas. This goes for you as a person as well, although you have already accomplished—or are in the process of accomplishing a major goal: establishing a professional career beyond just a day job. Learning to separate all your identities will allow for a healthier mindset and reduce a little stress. The last thing you want is to live your life in such a manner that causes you to look back in 10 to 20 years wondering who you are now or what happened to time. For my amusement, check or circle all that apply: Are you a,

- o Best friend?
- o Mom or dad?
- o Sports fanatic?
- o Sister or brother?
- o Husband or wife?
- o Community advocate?
- o Animal or reptile parent?
- o Fitness enthusiast or Couch potato (no judgement here)?

The goal is to recognize that you are more than just your career or status. Your achievements—no matter how significant—do not define your entire identity. Yes, you have accomplished something great, but that is a professional milestone, not the full measure of who you are. Your aspirations should extend beyond that: your dreams, visions, and goals set the tone.

With that said, let's dive into it: What are your goals?

Short term (within 1 year):

_____

_____

_____

_____

_____

Long term (within 5 years):

_____

_____

_____

_____

_____

**In this next set of questions,
dream as freely and boldly as you wish.**

What does your dream home look like? Include the driveway, amenities, property size, etc.

_____

_____

_____

_____

_____

_____

Where would you go on your dream vacation? Do you prefer a beachside retreat or a mountain escape? There are no limits—simply write down whatever comes to mind.

_____

_____

_____

_____

_____

_____

Consider the amount of money you would like to have, how do you envision financial security, and what risks you are willing to take.

Check all that apply.

- o Interested in learning about investments?
- o Do you want to build wealth that can be passed down to future generations?
- o Is creating generational wealth a priority for you?
- o Have you considered the dollar amount that would make you feel financially secure?
- o Are you familiar with terms: assets, liabilities, and passive income?
- o Have you considered retirement investment strategies in addition to a 401(k)?

I want you to fully understand that these questions are to get your mind open to possibilities of greater financial stability and are not beyond your reach, no matter where you are in life right now. Your past, family history, or environment does not determine your future or limit what you can achieve. Instead, it provides clarity on where you don't want to remain and helps you set the goals needed to move forward.

Setting aside any excuses, with the mindset of dreaming big—remembering, we mentioned: investments, generational wealth, the dollar amount you consider wealthy, and assets; Considering what those terms look like for you, what are your feelings on achieving financial freedom, Is it possible?

_____

_____

_____

Are there any obstacles you foresee that could stand in the way of achieving your dream goals?

_____

_____

_____

_____

_____

I'd like to take a moment to dive a bit deeper. I wrote a book, One Step, THE FIRST STEP, it's a guide on accomplishing everything in life by recognizing anything can be accomplished by focusing only on, THE

FIRST STEP. In the first chapter, we confront and come to terms with excuses. We learn that, in reality, everything we tell ourselves is just that: excuses.

Excuses on why we feel we cannot accomplish something through mentally listing reasons our goals won't come to fruition—thoughts like: I'm not smart enough, I don't know the right people, or I don't have the right look. These are all lies created by our mind's response to fear designed to "protect" us from the possibility of failure. This very response is what keeps us from pursuing what we truly want by planting seeds of doubt in our own minds. WE are the ones creating our own reasoning as to why WE cannot do something. That is silly. And, it makes no sense.

For a moment, revisit your responses from the question on page 14— the obstacles you foresee are holding you back from achieving financial freedom— the reasons you believe are standing in your way: Now, rewrite what you feel might hold you back from achieving your goals. I'll help you get started,

YOU!

That's it!! You are the only reason you cannot or will not move forward in life. Only you can change the way you think. Only you can choose to step forward with faith—or without it. Only you can wake up deciding you want more, then commit to having more.

When you first set out to become a Dental Hygienist, did you think it would be easy? That time would fly by? That you'd snap your fingers, and before you knew it you'd be making fifty dollars an hour while living a smooth and effortless life? No, you didn't! I'm sure you had countless questions racing through your mind—how to make it happen, the steps involved, and the financial aspect, just to name a few. Yet, even with life's challenges working against you, you either made it happen or are in the process of making it happen. Why? Because you decided then found a way to follow through.

It really is that simple.

And, achieving financial success—whatever that means to you—is no different. Make decision, follow through.

<u>Personal Goals and Dreams:</u>

I want you to write down your personal goals and dreams—but this time, without the limiting thoughts you once had. Be bold.

_____

_____

_____

_____

_____

_____

_____

_____

_____

_____

_____

_____

_____

_____

_____

_____

_____

_____

Career Opportunities

With a degree in dental hygiene, you have endless opportunities available to you. Whether you are seasoned or fresh out of school, your career isn't confined to working in a traditional office setting throughout your professional life.

If you're fresh out of Dental Hygiene School, don't be afraid to explore different work environments. You might consider spending your first year in one office then transitioning to a different-structured office in your second year. This will help you broaden your knowledge and adaptability early while gaining hands-on experience: Building a strong foundation in a variety of patient care settings while allowing you to develop essential skills and confidence is key for a successful career. This will also allow for ample time to decide what other opportunities you would like to explore, and possibly pursue.

For experienced hygienists who have been with the same office for many years, stepping outside your comfort zone can be intimidating but very beneficial: Working in a different office can introduce new techniques, new technology and help you break free from a stagnant or complacent work regimen.

When in the same environment for an extended period of time, people often become so comfortable with their daily routines it leads to a resistance to change—the mind shifts into a "protective" state, triggering fear of the unknown. Staying in the same place without setting new challenges can result in years passing with little financial and career progress to show for it. Which is why it's essential to set personal and professional goals at every stage of life. Growth requires change and embracing new experiences which then ensures continuous development professionally, and personally—not to mention, it helps avoid the "burn-out" phase mentally and physically.

With that said, don't be afraid to explore what I consider to be the exciting part of holding a dental degree—the diverse opportunities available to you as a Licensed Dental Hygienist.

A handful of Opportunity Options:

- ❖ **Temping.** Ranging from a single-day to several months, such as covering maternity leave. Some professionals choose to make temping their full-time career.

- ❖ **Teaching**. You can become an instructor:
  - o **Hygiene School**. Teach courses or take on an administrative role.
  - o **Dental Assisting School**. Same deal: Instructor or Admin role.

- ❖ **Military and Jails.** Civilian working for the government contract. Benefits:
  - o Competitive pay and excellent health benefits, along with a contract lasting up to five years.
  - o At the end of your contract, you have the option to renegotiate terms or conclude the agreement.

- ❖ **Event Speaker**. Continuing Education (CE) credit events feature guest speakers, including local events. Opportunities:
  - o Dental Labs
  - o Periodontists
  - o Oral Surgeons

- o Larger General Practices
- o State & County Associations

❖ **Traveling Hygienist.** In some states, you must work alongside a dentist, others you can operate independently. Look into your State Laws. To name a few positions:
  - o Hospitals
  - o Nursing homes
  - o Elementary schools
  - o Homebound patient care

❖ **Partnership.** You can own a portion of the practice by partnering with a dentist. The partnership can be a spouse or strictly a business associate.

❖ **Sales positions**. Just about everything in the dental office is supplied by a company, and most have Sales Reps. Opportunities:
  - o Loops
  - o Software
  - o Implants
  - o Toothpaste
  - o Technology
  - o Dental Suit Design
  - o Dental Instruments
  - o Product Distribution Companies

This is just to name a few sales opportunities. With your degree, you can pursue roles such as Territory

Sales Representative, District Sales Rep, or Regional Sales, including management roles. And Sales Reps earn substantial incomes—base salaries can go from 40,000 to over 100,000 plus you earn commission and should get a either a company car and phone or car and phone allowance and a slew of other perks. Don't let the "Sales" aspect of it intimidate you, It's about taking baby steps, embracing vulnerability, and overcoming the learning curve hump—just as you did in Dental Hygiene School.

Everything in life seems scary until you overcome the obstacles you fear. So don't be intimated by going for something new, worst-case scenario, it's not for you and that's ok: you always have clinical chairside to fall back on. Best case scenario, you absolutely love it, make bank doing so, and save your hands and wrist from excessive wear-and-tear. Until you put yourself out there, regardless what it is, you never know what possibilities could come of it.

This holds true as well—not putting yourself out there professionally guarantees to have detrimental effects on your bank account due to you being the type of person who accepts lower pay, doesn't fight for bonuses or benefits, and usually ends up working under the same doctor year after year wasting away their potential, and wrist mobility.

Getting back to opportunity options, after all these years, a Dentist-Hygienist Partnership Practice is still relatively rare. Yes, there are challenges and obstacles in making this work, but there are solutions to almost every problem in life. I am confident there are plenty of ways to make this legally viable with the correct approach and legal counsel; Therefore, do not limit your capabilities, and don't be afraid to pursue your goals, even if the goal is part ownership of a dental practice. Take the time to thoroughly read and understand your state laws:

- o What are you allowed to do?
- o What are you not allowed to do?
- o Can you administer Botox injections?
- o Are you eligible to administer nerve blocks?
- o What about working outside of the office, such as home visits without doctor supervision?

Understanding your state laws and obtaining as many certifications as possible will provide you with more leverage during hiring negotiations and give you the credentials to take your career to the next level—whatever that may look like for you.

Career Opportunities: Goals /To-Dos

What are your Dental Hygienist State Laws?

_____

_____

_____

_____

_____

_____

_____

Two opportunities mentioned of interest to you?

_____

_____

Are there any other certification you can get?

_____

_____

Game Plan

W e've discussed **Personal Goals**, **Life After Hygiene** goals, and some **Career Opportunities** you may not have considered before discussing here. Now, let's dive deeper into the details of your career and personal life's goals to create a plan for achieving the vision you set for yourself. The purpose of this is to use your goals as a guide for identifying actionable steps that will lead you to the financial outcome you're aiming for. Some of the content may seem repetitive, but we're refining it to create a clear, straight-forward path.

When writing your responses on the following pages, keep them concise and focused in this manner,

Examples:

Business Goals...
Short Term: Nerve Block certification
Long Term: Pursue a career in sales or teaching

Personal Goals...

Short Term: Join adult volleyball league
Long Term: Travel to Maui

What are your short-term goals?

Two short-term business goals:

_____

_____

Two short-term personal goals:

_____

_____

What are your long-term goals?

Two long-term business goals:

_____

_____

_____

Two long-term personal goals:

_____

_____

_____

Excuses set aside, is there anything you foresee holding you back from achieving these goals?

For example,

- Do you need further training or certifications?
- Are you business savvy or need to take classes?

Genuine Obstacles:

_____

_____

How is your mindset:

 Are you positively driven and goal-oriented?

_____

Do you self-sabotage with thoughts of doubt?

_____

_____

When working toward our goals, we often become so caught up in our daily routines that time slips away, and before we know it, a year has passed without us accomplishing anything.

For that reason, I want you to...

First, take a moment to briefly jot down a blurb about who you are: Where you are in life right now. What do you love? Who do you love? What are you passionate about? Do you have any hobbies? If so, what are they? And, finally, the month/day/year.

_____

_____

_____

_____

_____

_____

_____

_____

_____

_____

_____

"Authenticity is the daily practice of letting go of who we think we're supposed to be and embracing who we are."

- **Brene' Brown**

After taking a moment to connect with your most authentic self, I want you to rewrite your goals:

Where do you truly want to go in life? Who do you want to become? (both personally and professionally)

_____

_____

_____

_____

_____

_____

_____

_____

_____

Getting back to how I want you to start writing your goals, let's hone in on that clear and concise writing technique,

Business goal: Block injection certification
FIRST Step: Search for & enroll in a course near me

Personal goal: Join adult volleyball league
FIRST Step: Search for & join a league near me

Keep your goals simple at every step by writing down only the First Step. Get a dry erase whiteboard then place it on your bedroom wall using multiple colors to make it visually appealing; Also, keep the goal the same until it's accomplished—only changing the "First Step" portion. When you see your goals and the next step every day by having it in your face when you wake up, you are more likely to just do the task, thereby, leading you to accomplishing your goals.

Method is simple, erase the "First Step" then replace it with the next first step. In the example above, you would erase "Search for" and replace it with...

Business goal: Obtain block injection certification
FIRST Step:
Erase: Search for course & enroll
Replace with: Show up for course with date/time

Personal goal: Join adult volleyball league
FIRST Step:
Erase: Search for & join a league
Replace with: Go to the first game with date/time

Writing down the day and time, then set as many reminders on your phone as necessary to ensure you attend will keep you on track for accomplishing those goals. Once you attend the first session, you can erase those goals then set yourself up for the next set of goals. As we have previously discussed—everything in life is designed with the endgame in mind so you should know, Goal Setting is a lifelong process.

The day you stop setting goals, is the day your life is basically over—You no longer have a purpose.

With that said, the last thing I want you to do is to write down the very FIRST Step you can take to get the ball rolling. I'll help you get started,

BUY A DRY ERASE WHITEBOARD

If you already have one, perfect! Your actual final step is to rewrite your first business and personal goal in this simplistic manner on your whiteboard. If you tend to get overwhelmed easily, focus solely on one major personal goal, as this is the one that will give you the motivation needed to advance your career or increase your pay. It is your "WHY" and without a strong why, the attitude towards that goal becomes optional.

To start, write your goals here.

Business Goal: _____

First Step: _____

Personal Goal: _____

First Step: _____

When you utilize The First Step—Erase then Replace Method it blocks out all the noise and excuses, giving you one simple task to complete while keeping you actively taking actionable, forward-moving steps towards achieving your goals and visions. If you want to go the extra mile, write above the first step your "why" for wanting to achieve this goal using the same clear and concise tone.

Important because: _____

Business Goal: _____

First Step: _____

Then do the same with your personal goal. It sets the tone and creates the urgency. Make your why strong.

SECTION TWO:

Building Your Bank Account

SECTION TWO: BUILDING YOUR BANK ACCOUNT

SECTION 2

Investing In You

G etting accepted into dental hygiene school, completing it, then passing the state boards requires a lot of commitment, hard work, and discipline—adding the burden of student loans intensifies the pressure of the aftermath process which is why I always ask the same rhetorical question:

What is the purpose of all of this if you do not have anything significant to show for it?

Yes, you may make "good" money, but you're also paying off a "good" amount of debt. And the concept of "good" varies for everyone, in such that, you might feel earning forty-five dollars an hour is great money, while others may view it as barely enough to get by. What we all need to understand is that it's not how much money you earn that matters—it's what you choose to do with the money earned that makes the difference.

For example, you could earn one hundred dollars an hour, but if you choose to buy a big house, a fancy car, and other material items while paying off current debt, you're essentially working just to pay off the growing debt you keep accumulating. At that point, the amount of money you make doesn't matter if you remain trapped in the work-buy-debt cycle.

On the other hand, if you're earning twenty-five dollars an hour, living comfortably yet cautiously or frugally spending, and prioritizing paying yourself first (investing in your future, even if it's five dollars each paycheck), you'll always come out ahead.

It's like the story of the turtle and the hare: The hare makes fast (cheap) money and spends fast; The turtle makes slow (grow) money and spends slow. Who wins the race? The turtle!

Be The Turtle

Investing in You isn't just about money; it's about learning to prioritize your well-being. It's about understanding your worth, continuously improving to become the best version of yourself, and creating meaningful memories. Most importantly, it's about always learning and growing as a person. Living well doesn't have to mean living extravagantly—it could mean:

- Saving for vacation to create lasting memories.
- Buying fruits and veggies instead of processed food.
- Treating yourself to a fancy restaurant once a month.
- Owning a modest, reliable vehicle vs a fancy car
- Joining a $10-a-month gym rather than paying for an expensive membership full of amenities you'll never use.

The point is, you're using your money to support good health decisions, create lasting memories, and build special moments, all while living modestly to enable you to pay off debt faster—whether it's student loans, credit cards, car payments, or your mortgage.

It also allows you to save and invest in your future. Luxury will come in Divine Timing, but unless you have your checking account, savings connected to your checking, and your High Yield Money Market (interest-bearing savings) stacked, along with other investments that allow your money to work for you, then you have no business buying luxury, materialistic items of any kind.

Speaking of, let's chat about making money work for you and having "stacked" accounts. Again, it doesn't matter if you only have five dollars to save each paycheck. What matters is you making saving a priority and being consistent in your efforts.

Monthly bills: Home, transportation, electricity, phone, gas, groceries, car insurance (all must dos)

Extra expenses: Loans, credit cards, household stuff (necessities but non-essentials)

Extra spending: Morning gas station run, non-packed lunch, nails, cable (Luxury items)

Total monthly bills (Must pay): $ _____

Total extra expenses (non-essentials): $ _____

Total extra spending (Luxury): $ _____

Add all those up: $ _____

Total amount you make per paycheck? $ _____

For now, simply write down the totals. We'll dive deeper into this in the next chapter: Money In, Money Out. This is just a prep-step to help you adopt a money-conscious mindset and have a basic understanding of your financial status.

When learning about money, I always recommend a few starter books, and this time will be no different. Read the following in this order:

**The Richest Man in Babylon
by George S. Clason**

**The Automatic Millionaire
by David Bach**

If you've read both or are solid with the basics of your financials, I suggest switching gears and reading something that boosts you in other ways aside from money. Perhaps a biography of a motivational speaker or positivity-focused public figure—someone you admire who is in the financial or social position you aspire to reach. As we discussed earlier, investing in yourself is not only about financial matters, it's the bigger picture of continuously learning, growing, and becoming the best version of yourself—spiritually included.

I'll tell you this right now: say what you want, but if you're not aligned spiritually, you won't be aligned mentally, emotionally, physically, or financially. How does it all connect? Simple:

To overcome life's challenges, you must have a positive mindset.

To maintain a positive mindset, you must have Faith.

To achieve your goals, you must maintain a positive mindset, overcome challenges, and believe in your God-given abilities also known as, having Faith.

The deeper your Faith, the easier to relinquish your fears, worries, and concerns to your Creator. You don't have to bear the burden of trying to achieve everything on your own. You can move forward with confidence knowing that all things ALWAYS work out in your favor. Life IS working for you, not against you.

So again, **Investing In You** means having enough Faith to overcome those challenges that aim to keep you from receiving all the blessings in life that are awaiting your arrival. It also means knowing <u>who</u> you should invest in, keeping your inner circle very close and spending the majority of your free time investing in your immediate family, your community, and in ways that ultimately build you up—allowing your best self to shine.

A few suggestions for Free-Time Fun:

- Create a date night with the family (no phones)
- Take a bestie out to dinner
- Plan a self-care day
- Volunteer once a month
  - Church
  - Food bank
  - Animal shelter
  - Homeless shelter
  - Drug rehab facility
  - Become a Big Sister or Big Brother

...On the next page we will dive a little deeper.

Investing In You: Goals/To-Dos

What are a few ways you can create more meaningful memories with little cost?

_____

_____

_____

Reading is an incredible way to boost your morale, what is your next read on improving: self-worth, wealth, confidence, etc.?

_____

_____

_____

Additional Notes:

_____

_____

_____

_____

_____

_____

_____

Money In, Money Out

Money is simply printed paper cut into rectangles. Its value comes from the meaning you assign to it. The more you understand money, the better your relationship with money will be, and the more value it will bring to your life. The purpose of this section is to start learning about money—learn it, study it, read about it, and develop a healthy relationship with it.

There is a multitude of literature concerning financial matters, encompassing topics such as saving strategies, investment approaches, and any other subject of interest you may wish to investigate. Pick a topic, then commit to reading at least one book per quarter, in between reading, utilize other learning methods such as movies or documentaries—Money Explained on Netflix is remarkable, very informative. The objective is to develop an understanding of how money works and how to utilize it to your advantage. Once you have a good understanding of it, you'll begin to see that life always works out: Money always comes back to you—provided you maintain a positive outlook on both money and life.

Another book I highly recommend reading...

"The Psychology of Money"
By Morgan Housel

The concept of The Psychology of Money: Timeless Lessons on Wealth, Greed, and Happiness takes a deep dive into the behaviors and attitudes that affect financial outcomes. It's quite fascinating. And, is another great starting point for getting an in-depth look on how one should view money.

Circling back to the last chapter: Investing In You. We briefly chatted about your current financials to get a basic understanding of your: Money In and Money Out. Now, let's go a little deeper.

How much money is in your checking and savings?
Checking: $ _____ Savings: $ _____
Total for "luxury item" expenses? $ _____
Total monthly expenses, include must pay and non-essentials? $ _____

List out these extra spending items (non-essentials and luxury: gym, nails, gas station drink, cable, etc).

_____

_____

_____

_____

If needed, pick 3 you're willing to let go?

_____

_____

What is your total debt: home, car, credit cards, loan. List items and amounts then overall total.

_____

_____

_____Total debt: $_____

Which debt has the highest interest rate? _____

Which debt has the lowest total balance? _____

When it comes to paying off debt, weigh your options then choose the method that provides you with the greatest satisfaction. Insight on options:

➢ **Higher interest.** A higher interest rate means you're wasting more money simply to have the "privilege" of a company lending you money.

➢ **Lower Balance**. Some people choose to pay off the smallest balance first, then apply that extra money toward another debt balance.

Which debt will you pay off first? _____

How much will you consistently put toward paying off the balance each time you get paid? $_____

What about your savings, how do you save money? Do you save: randomly, by percentage, set dollar amount? _____

As mentioned in previous chapters, prioritize saving money (paying yourself first) before paying anyone else—even before covering your mortgage or paying off your debt. Developing the habit of setting aside your share of the money you earned by paying you first, as time goes by, and you begin earning more money, these habits will be firmly in place—making paying yourself first second nature.

Again, the purpose of these conversations is to make you money-conscious and help you learn the basics so you can move forward with healthy money habits. Then, turn the saving and investing process into something you enjoy, wishfully even grow to love. Otherwise, you develop a negative outlook on the subject, leading to spirals of:

- o Monday blues
- o Dreading payday
- o Lavish spending sprees
- o Feelings of hopelessness
- o Carelessly running up credit card debt

All of which are just a few examples: When you have a negative relationship with money, you inadvertently have a negative relationship with life. You start to think, "What's the point if all I do is work to pay bills?" or "I'm never going to get ahead." Which then spirals to a negative rabbit hole of unhappiness with your current job and life causing you to either give up saving money or start blowing your money. As you can guess, the spiral continues: everything at work bothers you, and soon, life itself does too. This may sound like an exaggeration, but it's not—it is 100% reality. That's the concept behind,

"The American Rat Race."

Let's remove ourselves from this cycle: From this moment forward, vow to yourself to learn as much as you can to develop a healthy relationship with money. As adults, we should have a clear understanding of our financial health. You should know:

- o The total monthly income.
- o The total monthly expenses.
- o The amount of debt you carry.
- o The exact amount you're saving.
- o The status of your emergency fund.

A few financial-health tips,

- ➢ You should have at least three months' worth of your total monthly expenses saved.
- ➢ Do not rely on your significant other's income, as it is not guaranteed.
- ➢ Start slow. Nothing in life is worth becoming overwhelmed.

- ➢ Read one chapter or one page a night on the subject of money.
- ➢ Focus on building your checking account first, then savings. After that, High Yield Money Market Account (interest-earning savings).

Most importantly, DO NOT seek financial advice from your friend group or non-immediate family members, UNLESS you have a very close relationship with someone who has substantial wealth. Otherwise, keep your financial matters to yourself. Think about it: How can someone teach you about managing money if their own finances are in disarray.

Side note: This applies to all areas of life, do not discuss: your goals, dreams, or aspirations with friends or family unless they share similar goals *and* take actionable steps toward achieving their goals. My suggestion is to read, attend seminars, and listen to speakers who have walked the path you're on and where you aspire to be. I like to say, "Move in silence."

Also note: Learning about money is never wasted time, whether you're young or seasoned, there is always room for growth; Otherwise, I'm sure you would not be working nor reading this book, you'd be off on some relaxing or wild adventure planning your next investment. But you are not, you are here. So wisely spend a little more time learning about money.

To sum it up: Control what you can: what you cannot control, leave in the hands of your Creator. Do your best each day, leaving tomorrow for tomorrow.

Today,

    I will maintain a healthy outlook on money.

Today,

    I will take one step toward learning about money.

"The best preparation for tomorrow is doing your best today."

-   H. Jackson Brown, Jr.

Money In Money Out: Goals/To-Dos

_____

_____

_____

_____

_____

_____

_____

_____

_____

_____

_____

_____

_____

_____

_____

_____

"Formal education will make you a living: self-education will make you a fortune."

\-   Jim Rohn

Running Your Business

The moment you received your Dental Hygiene License, you earned the title of Business Owner. You are now the CEO of your own career. You worked hard to gain the right to dictate how you would like your professional journey to unfold. You are in demand—a valuable strong suit, if you will—and you should carry yourself as such. Treating your career as a business will make you infinitely wealthier.

This is where all the work from previous chapters ties in to create your ultimate goal map, the road to no longer working for another person—you work for you. Whether you're just starting out or have years of experience, it's never too late to begin something new, especially when it comes to your financials and livelihood. The foundation of this map or goal sheet will guide your next steps, no matter where you are in your career.

First, let's establish two ground rules:

- [ ] NEVER become complacent
- [ ] ALWAYS put yourself first

Check those boxes. Make the promise. Write it on your sticky whiteboard in your bedroom. Whatever it takes to make that commitment real and to abide by it, DO IT. This is YOUR life. I will repeat...

What is the point of working your whole life if you have nothing substantial to show for it?

Given that your goals are set for *Life After Hygiene*, your *Personal Goals* are now clear, you have explored various *Career Opportunities*, laid out your *Game Plan*, discussed the importance of *Investing In You*, and you are now fully aware of your *Money In and Money Out*, the concluding question is,

How will you *Run Your Business* to achieve your retirement objectives?

- o Will you make a name for yourself among peers and colleagues by:
  - ▪ Attending speaking events
  - ▪ Becoming a speaker or researcher

- - Engaging with board members
  - Volunteering in your community
- o Do you need full control, such as in:
  - A partnership
  - A traveling hygienist
  - Through full-time temping
- o Will you remain as is:
  - Stagnant or complacent
  - Comfortable—same mundane day in and day out

How you choose to manage your business directly impacts the reflection of your bank account—your path to becoming financially free—and your personal and professional success. It is your life, the way I see it,

You can make one of two choices:

1. **<u>Simple choice</u>**: Collecting a paycheck.

Working to collect a paycheck often leads to sloppy spending and patterns of the typical hamster wheel cycle: Work>collect>payout. Nevertheless, this is a choice—No judgement here.

2. **<u>Challenging choice</u>**: Create a Vision for your life.

Creating a vision for your life takes discipline, making clear goals, creating a healthy outlook on money, and consistently fostering a positive mindset. All of which will lead to an overall happier life.

Both paths, simple and challenging, lead to an income, but they result in very different bank account outcomes. This outcome is shaped by every decision you make throughout your career. Again, not judging, it is your life, you can live it however you see fit— without having to explain yourself to anyone.

Afterall,

You are the CEO of your career.

Running Your Business: Goals/To-dos

Have a heartfelt moment with yourself:

Do you now see yourself as a business owner and the CEO of your career? _____

Do you now feel as though you are more in control of the way you want your life to play out? _____

What changes will you make moving forward in both your personal life and in business?

_____

_____

_____

_____

_____

_____

_____

_____

In the coming chapters, we will explore more ways to level up and Become Unstoppable. But first, we need to get into the nitty gritty of how to avoid working your whole life: Next up, Retirement Goals.

Retirement Goals

When it comes to retirement, you want to create enough multiple streams of income throughout your "working years" to sustain you for at least 20 years after you retire. YES, TWENTY YEARS. The reason being, we are not in control of when we leave this planet, nor can we predict who will be by our side or what income (or lack thereof) they may bring to the table. Therefore, just like in business, you are the only one who can control your financial future.

This is between you and yourself; Again, no judgment.

- o Are you making enough investments now to fund your retirement? _____
- o Is it growing in a direction to support you for 20 years afterwards? _____
- o What percentage of your pay are you giving yourself first? _____
- o Do you educate yourself about investing and achieving financial freedom? _____

Reading is always my go-to; However, podcasts, audiobooks, or YouTube videos are effective when commuting, at the gym and before you fall asleep.

Develop a solid understanding of money:

First, learn the basics. Understand the ins and outs of your finances at home, then implement a solid savings plan to prepare you for the next step.

Second, learn low-risk ways to make your money work for you with minimal effort. This includes higher-interest accounts that only require depositing money into them. I like to call this the "set it & forget it" method of generating interest-bearing income.

The foundation of this plan is that you've consistently saved a percentage of each paycheck. After building up your checking and connected savings account, you will not stop saving—it's a lifelong commitment to yourself; therefore, it's time to shift the account your money goes into. Once established, set auto deposits.

As with everything else, READ to learn the different ways to earn higher interest, then decide which suits you best.

Consider low-risk, higher-interest options like the following:

- o Certificate of Deposit (CDs)
- o Roth IRA, 401(k), Simple IRA
- o High Yield Money Market Account
- o Treasury Bonds: I-Bonds, EE Bonds

Note: Do not think you can jump straight into higher-interest methods of saving—it's a misconception. These accounts can cost you money: If you withdraw early, the account will not yield interest and you can be penalized or if your balance falls below its threshold, you will get charged fees. Both serve no purpose, which is why this is the second step.

If you did your due diligence, by now, you should have mastered the basics, thereby developing good financial habits indicating you're ready for the, **THIRD** step: Income-generating Assets.

As you grow your investment portfolio you can begin exploring riskier, but more rewarding income-generating assets, such as investing in: real estate, stocks, or starting a side business like an LLC. These types of investments are better discussed with professionals—accountant, financial advisor, broker, real estate agent, etc.—and definitely after significant research has been performed to see which appeals to you, what you are most comfortable diving into, and, certainly, before engaging in discussions with the above named professionals so you can hold an intelligent conversation, meaning you know what questions to ask then have a good understanding of the received answers.

My goal is not to overwhelm you, but to help you build a solid financial future through actionable steps leading to a multi-range investment portfolio:

Saving money > low-risk investments > Higher-risk investments

Moving on, take the numbers from Money In, Money Out—these are the essential figures. You should be fully aware of the totals for each of the following:

Bills:	$ _____
Non-essentials:	$ _____
Monthly Spending:	$ _____
Checking account:	$ _____
Savings account:	$ _____
Total monthly income:	$ _____

Monthly income (−) monthly expenses:

_____ = $_____

Now, we are going to flip an important component of this—how much you are investing in yourself. This is like a 401(k)-plan deduction that is taken out before you pay anyone else. As you know, contributions to your 401(k) are deducted before taxes; investing in yourself means paying yourself first, before anyone else.

What amount will you set aside for savings BEFORE paying your creditors? It doesn't matter if it is one dollar or fifty dollars, consistency is what matters, not the amount. As your career advances, your pay will follow thereby making more money, in turn, you will increase the amount you set aside—not increase your spending abilities.

The amount I will FIRST set aside for my future is

$_____

The goal is to build your checking account to cover your total monthly spending, plus an additional $500 for a cushion so you're not living paycheck to paycheck and can automate your bill payments. Once that goal is reached, the next goal is building your savings account, connected to your checking, to cover 3 to 6 months of your total monthly spending.

Total monthly spending + $500 = $ _____

Total monthly spend x 3 = $ _____

After you've saved enough to cover 3 to 6 months of expenses in your standard savings, the final step is to roll over any additional savings into a High Yield Money Market Account.

Side note: Basic savings account, while very liquid meaning you can access it immediately, offers virtually no interest. A High Yield Money Market account, on the other hand, offers interest rates of over 4%. As previously discussed, the key is that you need to leave the money in the account to earn interest, and then the interest will start earning more interest—making your savings, aka your money, work for you.

To make the purpose of saving make more sense:

➢ Keeping enough to cover the monthly expenses in your checking is to avoid living paycheck to paycheck by having your next month's bill money in place then automating your outgoing payments (set it and forget it).

➢ The extra $500 in checking is your cushion, preventing you from dipping into your savings. Your standard savings is to prevent you from dipping into your Money Market account.

➢ From there, continue saving until you have enough to open a High Yield Account. Add your checking account to the Money Market account to set direct transfers, then set up automatic monthly or bi-weekly transfers.

Getting back to it, using the example of total monthly expenses being $2,000, **Goals to Reach**:

✓ Checking: $2,500 (Monthly total plus cushion)
✓ Connected savins: $6,000 (total x 3)
✓ High Yield Money Market: $5,000 minimum

As your investment portfolio further expands to include: Treasury bonds, CDs, stocks, etc., they too must all remain untouched. The exception—stocks can be moved around, but only to other investment opportunities such as other stocks or you can use the money/interest earned to purchase larger investments (this is how you avoid taxes). If interested in learning more about it, READ.

The purpose of this whole section: Everything we've covered the last three chapters is to help you Build Your Bank Account for two sole purposes:

1. By understanding that saving and investing is how wealth is created *over time* and, how it all begins with mastering the basics: Investing In You. Plain and simple.
2. When all your finances are in order, stacked and automated, your mind is freed to focus on the other matters in life.

I'll end with this,

"Do not save what is left after spending, but spend what is left after saving."

-   **Warren Buffett**

Retirement: Goals/To-Dos

Ideally, what year would you like to retire? _____

What type of investments would you like to learn more about?

_____

_____

_____

_____

_____

_____

_____

My goal for you, with this chapter, was to embrace the concept of saving—perhaps even finding joy in it—and to know that building ample wealth for retirement, and possibly enough to leave to your children, is more achievable than you once thought.

My expectation is, as of today, you take actionable steps toward achieving your dreams by developing a positive mindset about money—and perhaps even discovering the satisfaction of saving it.

<u>Retirement Goals/Notes/To-Dos:</u>

_____

_____

_____

_____

_____

_____

_____

_____

_____

_____

_____

_____

_____

_____

_____

_____

"The question isn't at what age I want to retire; it's at what income."

- George
Foreman

SECTION THREE:

Becoming Unstoppable

SECTION 3

Building Your Network

Your brand is everything when it comes to your career. How you carry yourself. How you maintain your workflow. How active you are in your community. The educational content you provide. The quality of care you offer. All of these contribute to defining the brand you are building. If you want to take it a step further, consider building a professional Google page, website, or social media presence to enhance the brand you're creating for yourself. There are no limitations. You have the opportunity to build a remarkable community of dental hygienists and set the standard for how a business professional elevates their career.

Once you have a clear understanding of your brand and consistently carry yourself accordingly, it's time to take the next step in building your net worth by growing your network. I cannot stress this enough: DO NOT become lazy, complacent, or stagnant with your career. Work hard for 5 to 10 years, then you can coast a bit if you wish. Use this time to invest in you. Networking is a critical component of increasing your bank account—It is yet another method for providing access to opportunities outside the operatory. Don't be afraid of stepping into the "Big Girl" or "Big Boy" world: Learn to speak with others as equals, not as superiors.

Networking Opportunities:

> LinkedIn
> Dental Conferences
> Dental Conventions
> Volunteer opportunities
> Active Social Media pages
> Dental Hygiene Study Clubs
> Dental Hygiene Associations
> Local Periodontists hosting study clubs

The most successful hygienists continuously expand their networks by gradually adding to their resume' portfolio. Set time-bound goals. Choose the networking opportunities that resonate most with you, then get involved. Start by observing, then gradually move toward active participation. You can go at your own pace—following through is key.

If you are more of an introvert, start by joining an online group and attending one or two webinars each month. When you feel ready, participate in the discussions by asking thoughtful questions or sharing insightful, non-combative comments. If after giving the group a fair chance, it doesn't resonate with you, consider checking out their meeting schedule, I'm confident you'll find a topic of interest or check out another group.

If you are an extrovert or prefer an in-person learning environment, you may enjoy finding a local study club or event. Similarly, begin by attending, then, as you become more comfortable join the conversation. In-person events are often more engaging in that the host typically offers food, appetizers, or a selection of beverages, plus they provide excellent networking opportunities within your community.

From there, set goals based on your availability and what you intend on achieving. Aim to join a new group, association, or volunteer once a month, every other month, or quarterly, with a minimum of three per year until you become heavily involved in a few, then you can scale it back to one a year. Ideally, you'll prioritize this as much—if not more—than your personal social life. There is no reason you can't commit to networking at least twice a month, whether online or in person.

The purpose of this is to become comfortable with your peers and colleagues thereby interacting as equals and learning from them, as well as, to meet those who are in positions you aspire to reach. Yes, you will encounter people who you quickly realize aren't a good fit for you—don't shun them too quickly, it is often those people we learn the most from. They teach us how we do not want to be and how we do want to be. Both are equally important to learn.

On the other hand, you'll also meet people you admire or look up to, and these individuals might seem intimidating at first—The more intimidating they appear, the clearer it becomes they're the ones you should engage with. These are the people who will help build your confidence, provide valuable insights, and are often at higher career levels. Once you connect with them, you'll quickly realize that, in many ways, they are like you. May even resemble you.

This might not make complete sense right now, but once you start networking and interacting with your colleagues, it will become clear. Your goal is not only to grow your network but to expand your intellectual horizons through learning and growing as a professional and educator to your patients. Remember, there are no limits to your growth—You are the one steering your career and financial future; therefore, you have the power to decide how far your business journey goes.

"The way to develop self-confidence is to do the thing you fear and get a record of successful experiences behind you."

- William Jennings Bryan

Build Your Network: Goals/To Do

Network opportunity that appeals to you:

_____

_____

Volunteering opportunities:

_____

_____

Continuing Education Events near you:

_____

_____

Local Study Clubs:

_____

_____

What are your goals for this year?

_____

_____

_____

_____

_____

Patient-Focused Business

When you chose to work in a healthcare setting, you made the commitment, and took an oath, to ethically and compassionately care for each of your patients thereby treating them with the same dedication, attention, and mannerism as you would a beloved family member or developing relationship. Such as, in the beginning stages we tend to present our best selves, even with their imperfections, we work hard to make the connection meaningful through asking thoughtful questions to better understand their needs and wants, and we generally stay committed, even when it feels challenging, until we decide it no longer serves us.

Think of it like meeting someone you're attracted to: In the beginning, we tend to focus on being the best version of ourselves—happy, outgoing, and eager to make a positive, lasting impression. In those first interactions, we smile, laugh, are thoughtful, and courteous—anything to charm the other person. After the date, we often want feedback: What did they think? How do they feel? When am I going to see them again? We seek valuable insights so we know what to adjust and what to keep the same for our next encounter. Minus the physical attraction, all patients should be treated equivalently—Greeting them with a warm, welcoming smile, asking insightful questions to better understand their needs, following up to hear their thoughts and feelings about the visit, then scheduling the next encounter.

Yes, just like dating, there will be people you have to let go. But this should only happen after you have made every effort to provide the best possible care and consulted with the doctor for guidance. You must have a good understanding of the scope of care in which you can provide. For those patients you're teetering between keeping and letting go, do not try to be the hero, your pay and career is not worth it; Especially with patients who are on the spectrum. If you are not equipped, 100% comfortable or experienced in addressing and handling their needs and temperament—Do Not attempt care.

With that said, most of the following example's merit being dismissed as YOUR patient. The doctor may opt to take them on with cleanings or refer them to a specialty practice: This is up to the discretion of the doctor. Either way, set your boundaries.

A few major no-nos:

- ✓ **Physical abuse**: Hitting, spitting, violently grabbing
- ✓ **Repeated cancellations**
- ✓ **Unwilling to pay-repeatedly**
- ✓ **Extreme, irrational vocal outbursts**
- ✓ **Uncomfortable Sexual advancements**
- ✓ **Scope of care: Beyond your expertise or comfort zone**
- ✓ **Drug use: If you are unfamiliar with the signs and symptoms take a CE course.**

In regards to Scope of Care, as communicated, there will be patients whose needs go beyond your expertise and should be discussed with your doctor then possibly referred to a colleague who specializes in hospital cases or the unique needs of the patient: such as patients with blood disorders, severe autism, or other extreme developmental disabilities. Some young children may also fall into this category and would be more suitably referred to a specialist. These and abovementioned are just a few examples. A key aspect of people-centered care is knowing the needs of each patient through verbal communication, physical observance, and reviewing their medical history to determine the most effective individual approach.

Side note: While front office may vet patients, don't rely solely on that. You are the one holding the license. Most front desk staff began their career being hired with no to minimal experience then "trained" on the job. This training typically involves sitting with another person who was also hired with little to no experience, resulting in a "learn as you go" process. The problem with this approach is that you don't know what you don't know.

Have your own back with each patient. Carefully review their health history, perform thorough perio exams and charting, then create an individualized treatment plan tailored to their needs and goals. If a patient has seen the doctor prior to them seeing you, be sure to review their chart then conduct your own full examination and health history evaluation.

Once again, protect yourself by keeping in mind that the health history could have been gone over by an assistant who may or may not have received proper training. With that said, be sure to continuously maintain your knowledge and understanding of the medical side of dentistry: Drug interactions and how a medical diagnosis could affect dental treatment.

Aim to also discuss these topics each visit, with each patient:

- ➢ **Sensitivities:** water, cold, hot, metal, and any specific areas of discomfort.
- ➢ **Past dental experiences:** both positive and negative.
- ➢ **Upcoming significant life events:** Family photos, a wedding, holidays, graduation, and actively dating (whiteners or ortho potential).

> ➢ **Females:** Menstruating or expecting?
> ➢ **Smile goals:** What changes would they make to their smile if given the opportunity?
> ➢ **Family smile history:** Did their parents or siblings have dental issues?

These types of questions will determine how to move forward with individualize care. For instance, females menstruating or expecting tend to have oral hypersensitivity or they may have other dental health problems: Teeth loosing, oral tumors, dry mouth, or teeth erosion due to vomiting.

When it comes to the care of your patient, you must determine the amount of time needed to provide effective treatment. These questions don't have to be long or complicated. You can begin to incorporate them when confirming the appointment, as you are escorting the patient to their operatory, or for a more direct, intimate patient relationship— ask while in the chair: Just be sure to control the conversation to keep it pleasant but concise and stay on topic.

In the next chapter, we will thoroughly explore the genuine essence of value-based patient care: "The Stella Story." It's a real role-playing chat between myself and a good friend recounting a conversation we had discussing my goals for the dental industry— and, why I write for dental...Better "people" care.

Prior to, A few questions for ya:

How rehearsed are you with patients on the spectrum?

_____

_____

_____

Have you had any training courses on understanding temperaments and disabilities?

_____

_____

_____

Are you familiar with the signs/symptoms of various drug use? _____

<u>Patient-Focused: Goals/To-Dos</u>

Who confirms your patient appointments?

_____

Who keeps a short-list of for last minute openings?

_____

Who schedules your patient's next appointment?

_____

How much time do you need to provide effective care?

_____

Continuing Education needed for advance care:

_____

_____

Additional Notes:

_____

_____

_____

_____

_____

The "Stella" Story

I was having dinner with a dear friend when a passionate discussion arose—the dental industry. During our discussion, she inquired about my reasoning for writing about dental, prompting me to respond with a question of my own:

Let me ask you this, **when was the last time you went to the dentist, and for what?**

Her (Stella's response): "To get my teeth cleaned. It's been a while because it's painful. My teeth are sensitive. And I feel like they don't care or listen."

Her response opened the gates:

Me: What part of getting your teeth cleaned bothers you the most?

Stella: "The water and the scraping. And the way they treat you. It's like they don't believe you. No one seems to care."

(During this hypothetical conversation with her dental office, I played the role of each dental staff member while she answered as she generally would. My purpose was to make it relatable)

Making the first appointment:

Receptionist: Ms. (insert name), we have you scheduled for (day/time). Are there any concerns or fears you have about getting your teeth cleaned?

Stella: "Yes, the water squirter and the scraper thing"

Receptionist: Thank you for letting me know. I'll make a note of that for your upcoming appointment.

Me (to my friend): If the person setting up your appointment asked about your concerns, would that make you feel a bit more at ease?

She replied: "YES, it would."

Upon Arrival...

Receptionist: Hi, Ms. (insert name). Thank you for coming in today. I saw the notes about sensitivity to scraping and water. We've shared your concerns with your hygienist.

Receptionist (5 minutes later): Your hygienist is on time; (He or She) will be out at (insert time) to take you back. Would you like something to drink, a warm towel, or to use the restroom before we begin?

Me (to my friend): If the front desk reiterated your concerns, kept you informed about your wait time, and was courteous and thoughtful, would that help you feel more at ease?

Stella: "Yeah, it would."

Walking to the back with your Hygienist...

Hygienist: Hello, Ms. (insert name), my name is (insert name). I have read the notes, we have a new technique that I feel will make you more comfortable, but, before we get started, I want to make sure all your concerns are addressed.

Hygienist: After you brush your teeth at home, does swishing with water bother you?

Stella: "No, I use warm water and gently swish."

Hygienist: Great. What if instead of using the water squirter we do a gentle, warm water rinse after your cleaning to remove the gritty feeling: I can have a small cup ready at your preferred temperature; Would that work better for you?

Stella: "Yes, thank you. That would make me feel better."

Hygienist: Perfect. Now that we have a solution for your water sensitivity, may I ask about the sensitivity to scraping: My goal is to discover more solutions.

Are both the top and bottom teeth sensitive, or just certain areas? And, what specifically bothers you about the scraping?

Stella: "No, nothing on my lower teeth bothers me; It's just the two sides next to my front teeth, (she points to them). And it's the metal scraper."

Hygienist: Okay, perfect. I have a new plastic tool I can use for those sensitive areas, then switch to the standard instruments—very gently—for the rest of your teeth. I'll check in with you every step of the way.

Would it be okay if we try this approach to see if it makes you more comfortable?

Stella: "Yes, that sounds much better. Thank you!"

Me (to my friend): If your hygienist acknowledged your concerns about water and scraping—explained new techniques, asked exactly what bothers you, and discussed a solution—would that help you feel even more at ease?

She replied: "YES, it would!"

This role-playing, hypothetical conversation may sound familiar from my first book: Change A Smile, Change A Life, it's worth repeating many times over. This conversation demonstrates the value in being more attentive to patient's concerns simply through asking the right questions. It is a real-life example of how easily you can change a patient's perceptions of going to the dentist with a simple shift in communication—ask more in-depth questions, reword your explanations, and show patients that their concerns matter by having each team member become more attentive—this will drastically transform a person's mindset from fear and hesitation to confidence and comfortability. This also greatly increases the likelihood of patients scheduling their next appointment, leaving a five-star reviews, and addressing their other dental needs.

As for the front office, you may not initially have full control over how they operate, but a way to train them and to ensure patient concerns are acknowledged, is to simply ask:

"Did my patient mention any concerns?"

By consistently asking this question to the front desk staff they will in turn begin to ask your patients if they have any concerns due to becoming "tired" of saying, "I don't know." It is human nature to want to please. Thereby, consistently ask,

"Does my patient have any concerns?"

The day will come for the front office to automatically reply,

"Mrs. (insert name) is ready to be brought back. There are no concerns."

I promise you can train your front office staff without them even realizing it through consistency and repetition. The key: Train yourself first.

The other option: confirm your own patients either before ending your workday or in between patients. This eliminates the middleman, giving you better control over your schedule, your patients, and how smoothly your day unfolds. You can address concerns immediately or make a note in their chart, addressing it when in the chair or while walking them back.

Circling back to, "The Stella Story," dentistry has always been a very sensitive subject for many people. Some people absolutely love their dentist, others not so much. Very few are seemingly indifferent. Either way, one thing is certain—people are open to sharing their feelings about going to the dentist, especially the negative ones. Want proof, I challenge you to make a social media post asking for recommendations for a new dentist. And as you already know, dentist and their staff are often judged as a whole, in that, people don't tend to separate the individual roles within a practice—they refer to everyone under one name: The Dentist.

A few notable complaints on going to, "The Dentist"

"I hate going to the dentist. It's the worst pain ever."

"The receptionist is always rude when I check in."

"The person who cleans my teeth is too rough."

"They always charge so much: every time I go, I am told one price then before I leave it's another."

"I feel like I sit there FOREVER, then when I ask how much longer, no one gives me a clear answer—or they act rude. But if I'm late, they reschedule me."

"They never actually fix my problem. They hand me a prescription then have me come back in a few days."

" I feel like I am choking on water when I'm laid back. That sucky thing don't work."

! As an industry, we need to do better!

Patient Experience Improvements

I challenge you to ask 3 random people about their teeth-cleaning experience.

Person 1:

_____

_____

Person 2:

_____

_____

Person 3:

_____

_____

What can you do to improve?

_____

_____

_____

_____

_____

_____

Class It Up

As professionals, and adults we must carry ourselves with a sense of pride and professionalism. Many scrub-wearing personnel become lax in their appearance due to the daily routine of wearing scrubs. Without realizing it, they tend to choose scrubs purely based on comfort, laziness, or time-restraints: leaving the house in wrinkled, ill-fitting, mismatched, or faded uniforms. This unintentional habit can send the wrong message—one that suggests,

"My position is not important."

This applies to hygienists, dental assistants, CNAs, GNAs, front office staff, and, in some cases, even the doctor.

As human beings, when we take pride in our appearance before leaving home, we often feel more confident and prepared. Think about how transforming a neglected smile into a healthy, beautiful one can inspire someone to change their entire life. They go from barely opening their mouth when speaking to radiating confidence, their eyes bright with renewed energy. Their relationships improve, careers flourish, self-esteem strengthens, and their overall outlook shifts for the better. I have witnessed this countless times throughout my career. Dressing well has the same effect.

Looking better equates to feeling better.

Take pride in your appearance and represent yourself as a professional. Choose well-fitted scrubs made from quality material in flattering designs and colors. If your office provides uniforms, ensure they fit properly and are replaced when becoming stretched or faded. When attending a networking event, CE courses, or any professional gathering, wear business casual attire or a suit, depending on the setting. If you are attending after work, bring a change of clothes.

You are a High-Dollar Professional with a degree and license, act like it.

When you present yourself with confidence, your entire demeanor shifts. You stand taller, square your shoulders, shake hands firmly, and most importantly, recognize and feel your worth. This applies not just at work but in all areas of life—except Sundays. Sundays are for rest, relaxation, and resetting. Give yourself permission to enjoy guilt-free days doing absolutely nothing.

"The difference between ordinary and extraordinary is that little extra."

- Jimmy Johnson

Level Up Pro Tip: Personalized spaces in your home such as your bedroom or reading nook, your car, and your work space should be consistently clean and organized.

A cluttered room leads to a cluttered mind. Clear the room, clear your mind.

<u>Classing It Up: Goals/To-Dos</u>

Does your daily work attire, including shoes, make you feel confident or unconfident? _____

Do you have a few business-casual outfits and one well-fitted suit? _____

Are you intentional about how you present yourself in public? _____

What changes can you make to ensure you present yourself with confidence and professionalism?

_____

_____

_____

Name 2 professionally-dressed people you admire.

_____

_____

Is your home and work space clutter free? _____

What space(s) needs organization?

_____

_____

_____

Additional Notes or thoughts:

The Book in a Nutshell

I firmly believe that who we become, the goals we set out to accomplish, and the experiences we embrace all begin with **knowing who we are and what we want out of life** (Section 1: Building You). We then move forward with purpose.

You have chosen—or are on the path to becoming—a **Dental Hygienist**, that is no small achievement. Regardless if you worked full or part-time. balanced family responsibilities, or were able to pursue your education full-time, your journey required discipline, dedication, determination, and drive—all the D's. It was no easy feat. As with any major career path, the question remains:

What is the point if in the end, you have nothing to show for it?

And by "show for it," I am directly speaking of your financial success (Section 2: **Building Your Bank**

Account). Every decision you make in your career, and personal life, directly impacts your financial stability—your income, spending habits, savings, career growth, self-image, and the value you add to others. All of it reflects in your bank account.

The truth is, the only person you can fully rely on, especially in your later years is **yourself**. The choices you make today directly determine if your future is filled with security, or struggle and uncertainty.

When you set clear goals, define your ideal outcome, then take actionable steps to achieve those goals—while moving with integrity, maintaining your faith, and recognizing your worth—you are guaranteed to **Become Unstoppable** (Section 3).

The next question is:

What steps must you take to become the most exceptional and fulfilled version of yourself?

Simple answer:

Keep reading.

Keep learning.

Keep growing.

Keep building YOU.

"All our dreams can come true, IF we have the courage to pursue them."

- Walt Disney

A Guide to Running Your Dental Hygiene Business

A Special Thank You

Catholic Cathy–Dental Hygiene School instructor in Baltimore, MD. If it were not for your ignorance I would not of walked out. This walking out led to an incredible opportunity to begin my dental sales career.

Note: This is not to put down the Catholic religion: She reminded me of those old school mean teachers who hit children's knuckles with rulers.

Akua S., RDH – Felicity asked you to read my first book: Change A Smile, Change A Life (intended for Dentist), Your feedback, "It made me think. I don't like thinking." triggered me to think how neglected the Dental Hygiene Community is: leading to me writing this book. I'm so grateful for your feedback.

Which brings me to the most important shoutouts: My Girls, Felicity & Serenity.

Felicity–My Feisty Felicity, I am so extremely proud of you.

As you put it,

"The dental stuff is your passion, not mine. Why are you making me go into the dental field? I don't even like mouths."

Here you are, 6 years later, making a very good living for yourself as a Dental Assistant. And super exciting, taking your first prerequisites at CCBC with the goal of applying to their Dental Hygiene Program.

You are an incredibly caring, passionate assistant, I am confident you have a fabulous Hygiene career ahead of you.

Serenity – My Sweet Serenity. Passionate. Kind. Loving. The best friend to your AMAZING friend group anyone could ever ask for. I am so proud of you for choosing the Cosmetology Program as your High School Completer. Your ability to style and color hair is unmatched. I am so proud of the young woman you are becoming with such poise and grace. And, as of the writing of this book, your academic achievements: National Technical Honors Society and top 11% of your class. Shout out to Class of 2026!!

Love you Both

Acknowledgements:
Yasir Nadeem (Fiverr) – Cover art and design
Lucy S (Fiverr) – Editor-in-Chief @lucy_format
Your outstanding attention to detail, visual appeal, and contributions to my manuscript are deeply appreciated.

Keira R. – Deputy Editor
A special thank you to this young lady who has a very bright future ahead–Class of 2025. I wish you all the best on your next endeavor-College bound...whoot whoot! 🖤

A Portion of the Proceeds goes towards teeth care products for:

Lower Income Communities

Prostitutes (They need love too)

Shelters/Homeless

Recovering Addicts

Children in Need

Thank you for Your Purchase!

QR Code to purchase
Change A Smile, Change A Life

Open phone camera > hold camera up to image > a
link will appear on phone screen (Ingramspark)

($25.00 plus S & H)

More From the Author

A Book for Dental Practice Owners

Makes a wonderful gift for your Doctor (Dentist)

In this cleverly written, educational and inspiring book you will begin to develop the "Invest In Me and My Business" mindset pushing both your personal and business life to the next level.

Section One: Set Yourself up for Success sets the tone. Section Two: Tips and Tricks for Success builds your bank account. Section Three: Successfully Bowing Out create your why and gives you clear direction.

Get ready to deep dive into your dental soul and make a boat load of money!

QR Code to purchase
One Step, The First Step

Open phone camera > hold camera up to image > a
link will appear on phone screen (Ingramspark)
Available in the UK and USA

($15.00 plus S & H)

A book for the everyday person who wants to enrich their life

As we navigate life, we often find ourselves between staying authentically true to ourselves and people-pleasing. Letting go of excuses, taking accountability, and simplifying our goals comes down to: One step, The First Step: Putting Yourself First.

On this slightly scary, educational, and impactful journey, you will learn how to differentiate between friend & foe, overcome financial illiteracies, and what accountability really is: all while achieve everything you want in life by embracing the power of one simple yet profound concept:

The First Step is the ONLY Step.

A Guide to Running Your Dental Hygiene Business

www.ingramcontent.com/pod-product-compliance
Lightning Source LLC
Chambersburg PA
CBHW050443150626
46551CB00028B/1232